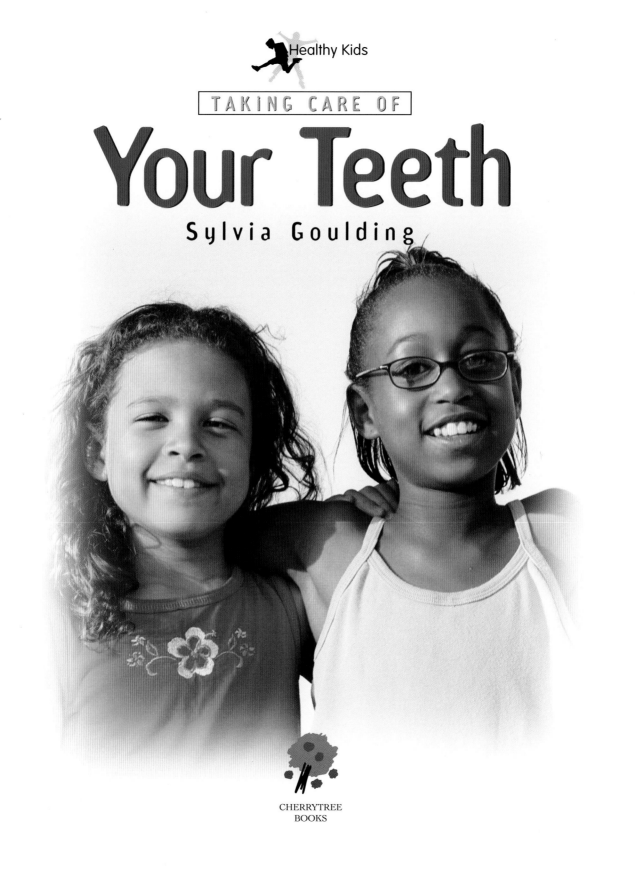

Healthy Kids

TAKING CARE OF
Your Teeth

Sylvia Goulding

CHERRYTREE
BOOKS

Published in 2006 by The Evans Publishing Group
2A Portman Mansions
Chiltern Steet
London W1U 6NR

Printed in China

British Library Cataloguing in Publication Data

Goulding, Sylvia
  Taking care of your teeth. - (Healthy kids)
  1.Teeth - Care and hygiene - Juvenile literature
  I.Title
  617.6'01

  ISBN-10 paperback: 1842343165
  ISBN-13 paperback: 9781842343166
  ISBN-10 hardback: 1842344102
  ISBN-13 hardback: 9781842344101

PHOTOGRAPHIC CREDITS
Cover: **The Brown Reference Group plc**: Edward Allwright; **BananaStock** (bottom right); **Gareth Boden** (bottom left)
Title page: **BananaStock**
BananaStock: 5, 13, 28; **The Brown Reference Group plc**: Edward Allwright 3, 4, 5, 6, 7, 8, 9, 10, 12, 14, 15, 16, 17, 18, 20, 24, 25, 26, 27; **Hemera Photo Objects**: 13, 19; **Simon Farnhell**: 9, 12, 17, 18, 19; **Photos.com**: 21.

FOR THE EVANS PUBLISHING GROUP

Editor: **Louise John**
Production: **Jenny Mulvanny**
Design: **D. R. ink**
Consultant: **Dr. Julia Dalton BM DCH**

FOR THE BROWN REFERENCE GROUP PLC

Art Editor: **Norma Martin**
Managing Editor: **Bridget Giles**

With thanks to models **Natalie Allwright, India Celeste Aloysius, Molly and Nene Camara, Daniel Charles, Zac Evans, Isabella Farnhell, Jordan and Connor Thorpe, Sam Thomson, Joshua and Callum Tolley, and Isabella Trevisiol**

Important note: Healthy Kids *encourages readers to actively pursue good health for life. All information in* **Healthy Kids** *is for educational purposes only. For specific and personal medical advice, diagnoses, treatment and exercise and diet advice, consult your doctor.*

Some words are shown in bold, **like this**. You can find out what they mean by looking in the glossary on page 30.

Contents

Perfect teeth

Our teeth do many jobs. Without them, eating is difficult. Teeth bite or tear food. They slice it and grind it. They stop us dribbling. They are also one of the first things people notice when we smile. Teeth even help us make certain sounds when we speak. But teeth need good care. If you don't look after them, they start to rot. You'll need fillings. Or the dentist may have to pull a tooth out. Better clean them now!

◀ *Look after your teeth and keep them gleaming white and healthy for life.*

Or try this...

Feeding your teeth...
- Avoid sticky foods – brush right away.
- Chew fresh, crunchy vegetables.
- Eat dairy foods – milk, yogurt, cheese.

Protect your teeth...
Stop your teeth being knocked out. Wear a mouthguard when you play contact sports like boxing, rugby or hockey.

Keeping your teeth perfect

Good brushing
Brush your teeth in the morning and evening. Floss between your teeth so no food stays behind. It's the only way to keep teeth healthy. Change your toothbrush every three months.

Visiting the dentist
Get your teeth checked. Visit the dentist every six months and when you have a toothache.

Avoiding sweets
Try not to eat sweets or drink sugary drinks. If you do, make sure you brush your teeth carefully afterwards.

◀ *No sweets in bed! They will rot your teeth and give you toothache.*

▶ *Smile at the people you meet and they will smile back at you.*

Just amazing!

What a mouthful!
The giant armadillo has about 100 teeth. But the long-snouted spinner dolphin has even more: it boasts 252 teeth!

Types of teeth

the teeth at the front of your mouth are a different shape from those at the back. This is because they do different jobs. Your teeth include knife-sharp **incisors** that bite and slice. Pointed **canines** stab and tear. Large, flat **molars** grind and crush your food. Adults also have premolars between their canines and molars. Grown-ups have extra molars called wisdom teeth.

◀ *Take a bite out of a pizza. Which teeth do you use? Your front teeth, or incisors, help you slice through the pizza dough.*

Just amazing!

What's for dinner?
Each animal's teeth are right for the food it eats. Sheep have no incisors in their upper jaw. This makes it easier for them to pull out grass. Squirrels, however, have large front incisors that bite through hard nuts. People eat both meat and plants, so we have different kinds of teeth.

Your first teeth

Incisors at the front

You have eight incisors – four in your upper jaw and four in your lower jaw. Incisor means 'biting tooth'. Incisors have sharp edges that help you bite or slice food, for example a slice of pizza.

Canines in the corner

You have four canines – two in the upper and two in the lower jaw. The canines sit either side of the incisors. Canine means 'like a dog'. We use these teeth to stab and tear food.

Molars

You have eight molars – four in the upper and four in the lower jaw. These flat teeth in the back of your mouth help you grind your food to a pulp.

▶ *You can clearly see all the teeth in this boy's upper jaw. He's already got most of his grown-up teeth.*

incisor
canine
premolar
molars

incisors
canine
premolar
molars

Just amazing!

Just teething!
● Some snakes have hollow teeth called fangs. Fangs pierce skin and inject poison into flesh.

Losing your baby teeth

When you are about six years old, your first teeth start to drop out. First one tooth gets wobbly. It rocks and feels loose. After a few days, it drops out. It could take six years before all your first teeth have gone. They are pushed out by a second set of teeth – your grown-up teeth. You have 20 first teeth but 32 grown-up teeth.

◄ *First a tooth wobbles. Then it might hang by a thread. Finally it drops out. Soon the one next to it follows.*

Or try this...

Getting rid of a wobbly tooth...
- Bite on a crusty piece of bread.
- Gently rock it with your tongue.
- Eat a crisp apple or a carrot stick.

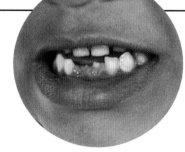

◄ *Can you see the adult teeth starting to grow? They pushed the baby teeth out.*

When they go...

Wobbly tooth

First, you feel a gentle rocking. Your tongue starts playing with your tooth. The rocking gets stronger. The loose tooth looks longer than the ones next to it. Suddenly – it has come out!

Painful gums

At first your gum feels a little sore where the tooth has come out. It could even bleed a little bit. If so, push your tongue into the gap.

A new tooth on its way

Soon you can see a tiny white spot. It feels sharp on your finger and your tongue. It is the first corner of your adult tooth pushing through.

▶ *If the tooth fairy finds a baby tooth under your pillow, she may take the tooth and leave a coin.*

◀ *Some children keep their baby teeth in a special box.*

Just amazing!

Second teeth, third teeth...

Throughout its life, the shark grows new teeth. As soon as one tooth drops out, a new one takes its place.

▶ *For a few years, you'll have some baby teeth and some adult teeth.*

Inside teeth

each tooth is made of several layers. The outer layer is shiny **enamel**. That's the hardest material in your body. Even so, the tiny germs that help break down your food also attack the enamel. If you don't keep your teeth clean, the enamel cracks. The germs can then get inside your teeth and rot them.

◀ *Enamel makes your teeth hard enough to bite a hard biscuit. But if you eat lots of biscuits, they'll crack your enamel.*

Just amazing!

Don't try this at home...
A Belgian man has the strongest teeth. He pulled two train carriages with a rope held between his teeth.

Worn out...
A rat gnaws all the time to wear down its front teeth. If it doesn't, the bottom teeth grow straight up into its brain.

What is it?

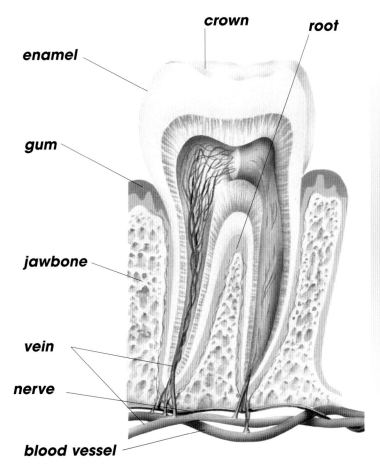

crown

root

enamel

gum

jawbone

vein

nerve

blood vessel

Crown The part of your tooth not covered by the gums.

Gum Soft, pink flesh around teeth.

Enamel Hard outer layer of teeth.

Bone The jaw is a bone. Your teeth sit in hollows in that bone.

Root The part of a tooth you can't see under the gum. The tooth is 'anchored' with roots, just like a plant in soil.

Nerve There are **nerves** inside teeth. They make you feel pain if you have a rotten tooth.

Quiz -?-?-?-?-?

1 Teeth are covered in enamel...
A ...so you can break up food.
B ...to make your teeth sharp.
C ...to protect the inside of the tooth.

2 Teeth have roots...
A ...to hold them firmly in position.
B ...to give you toothache.
C ...so the dentist can pull them out.

Answers: 1A and C, 2A

Which brush?

there are lots of different toothbrushes. Choose one that you can comfortably hold in your hand. A small head with soft or medium bristles is best. If the bristles are very hard, you could scratch the enamel of your teeth. Electric toothbrushes are great to use. They have small round heads that **rotate** on your tooth. All you do is hold the brush where you need to clean.

◀ *There are lots of exciting toothbrushes. Some have pictures of popular TV characters on them.*

Do this...

Toothbrush know-how
- Do replace your brush or the head of the electric brush every three months.
- Do rinse your brush thoroughly.

Don't do this...

- Don't share your toothbrush with anyone.
- Don't chew on your brush.
- Don't use a frayed brush.

All sorts of brushes...

Children's toothbrushes

There are different types of brushes for younger and older children. When you have all your first teeth, and some second teeth are starting to come through, use a stage 3 brush. When you're eight years or older, use a stage 4 brush.

Electric toothbrushes

Don't miss any teeth. Hold the brush where you normally brush. Brush the gums, too. Change the brush head every three months.

Brush facts

▲ *Put a blob of your favourite toothpaste on the brush. But don't swallow the paste.*

▼ *Always start in the same spot so you know which teeth you've cleaned.*

1 use small soft brushes

rinse the brush after brushing

Just amazing!

In some parts of Africa people clean their teeth with twigs. The chewed, frayed end of a shea tree twig makes an excellent brush.

get a new brush every 3 months

13

How to brush...

you might think that everyone knows how to brush their teeth. But most people don't brush well enough. Each brushing session should take about three minutes. But many people brush for just 30 seconds. Clean your teeth in the morning and in the evening. Brush after a meal or after eating sweets, too. It's important to get every bit of food out of your mouth, especially sugary foods.

◀ *Freshly brushed teeth feel good. Your teeth look sparkling clean. You have a fresh taste in your mouth, too.*

Safety first!

Don't brush too hard!
You need to brush your teeth carefully. But don't attack them. Too much force could damage the tooth enamel.

Healthy teeth, healthy body...
Severe tooth and gum problems could lead to heart disease, blocked blood vessels, and stroke. So keep brushing!

Toothbrushing step-by-step

Get your toothbrush ready
Put toothpaste on your brush. You only need a small blob the size of a pea.

Brush the front of each tooth
Carefully brush the front of each tooth *(see the picture on page 14)*. Always start with the incisors, then do the canines *(see step 1)* so you know which teeth you have brushed. Don't forget the molars *(see step 2)*.

Brush back and top of each tooth
Open your mouth wide and brush the back of each tooth. Then brush the cutting surfaces of your teeth *(see step 3)*. Brush for three minutes in all.

Floss between your teeth
Once a day, floss your teeth *(see pages 16 and 17)*. Also floss if there is food stuck between your teeth.

Rinse your brush
Wash out your mouth with cold water. Rinse your toothbrush.

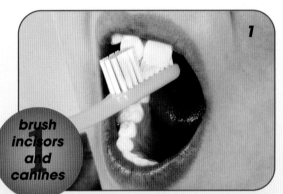

brush incisors and canines

brush the molars

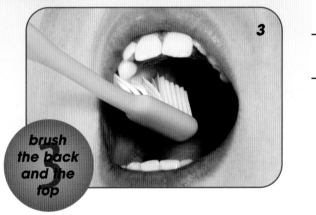

brush the back and the top

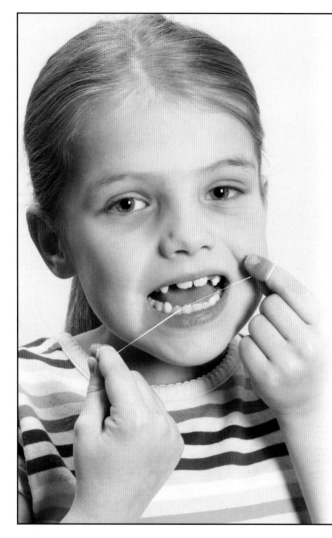

Flossing
Why is it important?

flossing is the best way to prevent gum disease. If you use only a toothbrush to clean your teeth, you won't be able to clean everywhere. Dental floss is a thin nylon thread. The thread is wrapped around a spool. Floss helps you reach places that your brush can't. The thread can reach the spaces between your teeth and get closer to the gums. Floss your teeth really clean!

◄ *Tear off a length of floss. Wrap each end around a middle finger. Pull the thread back and forth between your teeth. Be very gentle so as not to hurt your gums.*

Or try this...

How to clean your teeth when you haven't got a toothbrush or water...
● Carry a spool of floss with you so you can always clean between your teeth.

● Chew some sugarfree gum. It makes saliva in your mouth. Saliva helps get rid of some germs.

Perfectly clean

Flossing

Floss once a day. The best time to floss is the evening. Eat, then brush your teeth, then floss. Don't eat or drink anything afterwards.

Water picks

If you don't like flossing, try a water pick. It sends out a thin jet of water that picks out food remains.

Disclosing tablets

You can buy these pink tablets at a pharmacy. After brushing your teeth, chew one for a few minutes, then spit it out. The red stains show where you have not cleaned properly.

▶ There are many types of floss. Some are very thin. Some, like dental tape, are wider. Some taste of mint.

dental tape
waxed
30M

PLAQUE CHECK
DISCLOSING
TABLETS
PL 1424/0018

BN. 17058
EXP. 04-06

◀ Chew a disclosing tablet to check your toothbrushing.

Just amazing!

Drown the germs...

Germs love a dry mouth. Drink plenty of water to wash away leftover foods. It leaves nowhere for germs to hide!

▲ ▶ Disclosing tablets stain your teeth red where germs hide.

Which foods are...
Good or bad?

We all have healthy germs in our mouth. They help us break down food. But germs can get out of hand. They live in a white, sticky layer on your teeth called **plaque**. Germs make **acid** from the sugar we eat. Acid then attacks the enamel and makes holes in it. Germs can get inside your teeth through these holes. Once inside, germs rot your teeth.

◀ *Chocolate sticks to your teeth and makes them rot.*

Do eat this...

Food that's good for your teeth...
● Chew fresh, raw vegetables like carrot sticks. The saliva in your mouth helps wash out food remains and germs.

● Eat and drink food rich in **calcium** and **vitamin D** to make teeth strong: milk, yogurt, cheese, oily fish and eggs.

Bad for your teeth

Sugary food and drink

All sweet food and drink can rot your teeth. Avoid biscuits, cakes, sweets, chocolate, sweet breakfast cereals and cereal bars and also fizzy drinks.

Sticky food

Some food is so sticky it's hard to get off your teeth. Chocolate and honey are particularly sticky.

Snack food

Children who snack between meals often don't brush their teeth. Sweets and crisps have all day to rot their teeth.

▲ *Apples are great. They make you chew. This makes your mouth water. The saliva cleans your teeth.*

Doughnuts are tasty, but they rot your teeth. It's best not to eat them, or brush afterwards.

Quiz -?-?-?-?-?

1 Which foods are good for your teeth?
A A chocolate bar and a fizzy drink.
B Carrot sticks and a piece of cheese.
C A snack of tortilla chips and dips.

2 After eating chocolate, you should...
A ...brush and floss extra carefully.
B ...eat some more chocolate.
C ...go to the dentist immediately.

Answers: 1B, 2A

What happens to...
Bad teeth

if you don't brush and floss properly, you'll soon know about it! Your teeth look dirty. Germs breed in your mouth. Your breath smells. Your gums bleed when you brush your teeth. Your teeth hurt because they have holes. The insides of your teeth start to rot. If you don't get treatment quickly, your teeth may even fall out!

◄ *Do your gums bleed when you bite into an apple? That's a sure sign of gum disease.*

How to tell...

Signs of gum disease
- bad breath or a bad taste
- red, swollen or bleeding gums
- loose teeth or pus between teeth

Signs of tooth decay
There are no nerves in the enamel. You can't feel a hole. A toothache tells you that tooth decay has already set in.

What can go wrong...

Plaque A white, sticky layer that builds up on your teeth and between the teeth and gums. It's the place where germs hide and breed.

Tartar Plaque hardens and becomes **tartar**. It's so hard you can't brush it off. The dentist has to chisel tartar off with special tools.

Dental caries **Dental caries** set in when your teeth get holes, called **cavities,** in them. Germs can get into the holes and rot the tooth.

Gum disease Your gums get sore and bleed. They shrink away from your teeth. More germs settle in the gaps. Your teeth get loose and drop out.

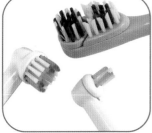

◀ *Special brushes can help you fight plaque.*

Tooth decay from bad toothbrushing is one of the most common children's disease in the United Kingdom.

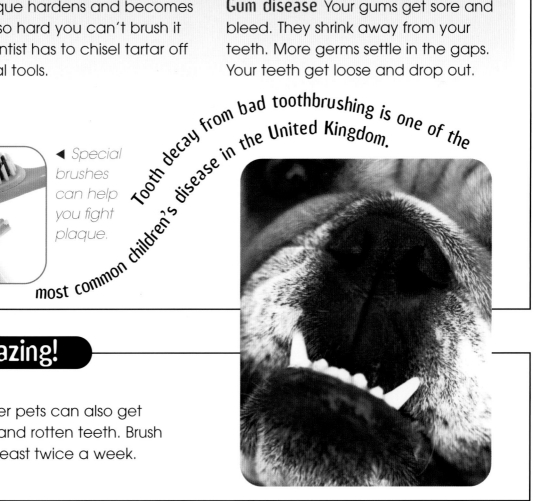

Just amazing!

Doggy teeth...
Dogs and other pets can also get dental caries and rotten teeth. Brush their teeth at least twice a week.

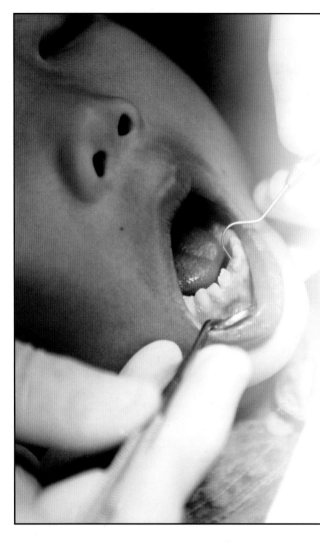

A visit to...
The dentist

even if you don't have toothache you need to visit the dentist twice a year. The dentist can check if your teeth are healthy. She can see the back of your teeth or take an X-ray of the root. She can treat problems. She can give fillings or pull out a tooth. Teeth stay healthy longer if you stop tooth decay and gum disease early.

◄ *The dentist pulls away your lip with a mirror to see the inside of your mouth. He prods the spaces between teeth with a metal hook.*

Dental jobs...

The dentist...
...checks for signs of tooth decay or gum disease, takes dental X-rays, gives fillings and takes out teeth if necessary.

The dental hygienist...
...scales, polishes and teaches cleaning.
The orthodontist...
...fits braces to correct crooked teeth.

What may happen

Check-up
The dentist checks each tooth. She also checks if your gums are healthy.

Cleaning
The dental **hygienist** removes plaque and tartar from your teeth. This is called **scaling**. If you have gum disease, he cleans the gums. Then he polishes your teeth.

Dental X-ray
An **X-ray** shows if the roots of your teeth are healthy.

Filling
If you have a cavity, you may need a filling (read pages 26 and 27).

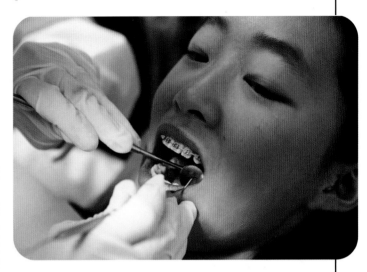

▲ *The **orthodontist** fits braces to straighten your teeth.*

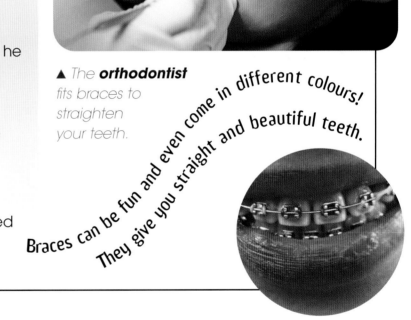

Braces can be fun and even come in different colours! They give you straight and beautiful teeth.

Smile!

Good teeth nation...
The number of school children in the UK who have tooth decay is lower than it has been for many years. More than three-quarters of all children say they brush their teeth twice a day and regularly visit the dentist. That's a good enough reason to smile!

When you have ...
Toothache

toothache can be one of the worst pains you ever get. It gnaws, throbs and niggles at you. You can't stop thinking about it. Take a painkiller to stop the pain. But it won't cure the problem. The most common cause for a toothache is dental caries, or a cavity. Get to the dentist as soon as you can. If you don't want toothache ever again, brush and floss properly!

◀ *Toothache can really get on your nerves. It's very painful. It can make your cheek red and swollen.*

Or try this...

Instant toothache help...
- Wash your mouth out with warm water.
- Rub the painful gum with oil of cloves.
- Drip some clove oil into a cavity.

▶ *Try placing an ice pack or a cold-water bottle on your cheek.*

What causes a toothache

Food stuck in your teeth
Wash it out with warm, salty water.
Use floss to get it out.

Dental caries
If you have a hole in your tooth, the
dentist needs to give you a filling.

An abscess
An **abscess** is a painful swelling of
the gum. The swelling contains pus.
Abscesses are caused by decayed
teeth that get **infected**.

To avoid toothache brush and floss twice every day.
Have a dental check-up twice a year.

▶ *You may feel a
sudden, stabbing
pain in your tooth
when you eat
something very
cold like an
ice cream.*

Safety first!

Call the dentist immediately if...
- ...your temperature is 39°C or more.
- ...your face is swollen.
- ...the pain is very strong or you feel sick.

If you need...
A filling

a cavity is a hole in a tooth. Germs have combined with sugar to make acid. The acid has made a hole in the two top layers of your tooth. Germs and bits of food can get into the centre of your tooth. It's only now that you start feeling toothache. You need to see the dentist as soon as you can. She will clean the hole and fill it.

◄ *The dentist swabs your gum to make it numb. This means he rubs it with anaesthetic. Now you won't feel the needle.*

Just amazing!

Goldentooth
In the past, dentists used all sorts of things to fill cavities: cork, gum, tin foil, gold leaf, lead and even stone chips.

► *Your gums will feel numb for about an hour after a filling.*

What happens...

Numbing the gum

First the dentist swabs the gum next to the painful tooth. It makes the gum **numb** so you can't feel pain.

Giving an injection

Now she pushes the needle in your gum. She **injects** a local **anaesthetic**.

This makes the nerves inside the tooth and the area around it numb.

Drilling and filling

Next she drills out the decay in your tooth. Then she plugs the empty hole. For this she uses either a silvery metal or a white plastic material. A filling will only take about 15 minutes.

▶ *After giving you the anaesthetic, the dentist drills into the cavity to get all the rotten bits out of the hole.*

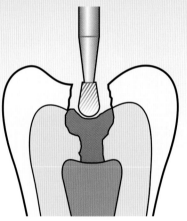

▶ *The dentist cleans the hole with a liquid that kills germs. Then she plugs it with a metal or plastic filling.*

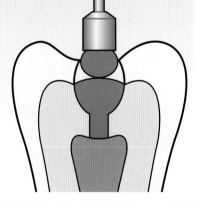

Or try this...

After the filling...
● Your mouth feels numb for an hour.
● Don't eat anything for two hours. Drink with care – you could dribble!

● When the anaesthetic wears off, you can feel your cheek and gums again. Your mouth may feel sore for a little while.
● Brush the filled tooth carefully at first.

Keep smiling...

It's easy to keep your teeth clean and healthy. It doesn't cost much money. It doesn't take very long. All you need is six minutes every day for cleaning, and 30 minutes a year to see the dentist. It's time well spent because your healthy teeth will stay with you all your life.

◄ Smile and show your gleaming teeth. Treat them well and you won't have to fear the dentist.

Just amazing!

Dental talk

You need your teeth not just for eating, but also to speak. Together with your tongue and other parts of your mouth they help you make sounds such as 'th' and 'd'. Try saying 'dentist' and 'teeth' very carefully. Can you feel your tongue playing against your teeth?

Test yourself

1. To clean your teeth, you need...
A special dental tools
B a toothbrush, toothpaste, water and dental floss
C a drill and cleaning fluid

2. What are canine teeth?
A They're four teeth between your incisors and premolars or molars. They help you stab and tear food.
B Only dogs have canine teeth.
C Only people who eat meat have canine teeth.

3. First teeth fall out because...
A ...they are worn out.
B ...we don't brush them properly.
C ...they need to make room for our second, or adult, teeth.

4. A cavity is...
A ...a hole in a tooth that needs a dental filling.
B ...the hole left in the gum when a baby tooth drops out.
C ...a type of dental filling.

5. Which food should you avoid?
A cheese, milk and yogurt
B crunchy fruits and vegetables
C sweet foods
D sticky foods

6. How many first teeth do you have?
A 54
B 32
C 20

ANSWERS: 1B, 2A, 3C, 4A, 5C and D, 6C

Just amazing!

Smile, please!
Scientists say there are 50 different smiles. They can tell if your smile is genuine or fake from the face muscles you move.

Famous smiles...
● the Mona Lisa, a famous painting
● the Cheshire Cat in *Alice in Wonderland*
● the smiley email symbol ☺

Glossary
What does it mean ?

abscess: *A swelling in the gum that is filled with pus (yellow, sticky fluid).*

acid: *A chemical, usually with a sour taste. It can damage tooth enamel and allow germs into our teeth.*

anaesthetic: *A drug that makes the body, or a part of it, unable to feel pain. The dentist uses an anaesthetic before filling a tooth or pulling it out.*

calcium: *A chalky substance in some foods, especially milk products. It is necessary for healthy teeth and bones.*

canine: *One of four pointed teeth, used for stabbing and tearing food.*

cavity: *A hole in a tooth caused by tooth decay. It needs filling.*

dental caries: *Cavities in your teeth.*

enamel: *The hard, white, shiny layer covering teeth. Unhealthy teeth have yellow enamel.*

hygienist: *A dental hygienist scales and cleans your teeth and teaches you how to brush and floss your teeth properly.*

incisor: *One of eight sharp teeth at the front of the mouth. We use them to slice and cut food when we bite into it.*

infected: *When germs cause disease or swelling, such as dental caries or abscesses.*

inject: *To use a hollow needle to put a medicine into the body.*

molar: *One of the large, flat back teeth. We use them for crushing and grinding food.*

nerve: *A bundle of fibres that sends messages from any part of the body to the brain. Nerves make you feel toothache.*

numb: *A part of your body is numb when you cannot feel anything. Your gums are numb after an anaesthetic.*

Visit these websites...

● www.dentalhealth.org.uk
British Dental Health Foundation website, offering advice on all aspects of dentistry.
● www.learnenglish.org.uk/kids/songs/toothfamily.html

orthodontist: *An orthodontist fits braces and straightens crooked teeth.*

plaque: *A sticky white material that forms around our teeth. Germs make plaque.*

rotate: *To turn around in one spot. The head of an electric toothbrush rotates.*

scale / scaling: *To remove hardened plaque from teeth with special tools.*

tartar: *Plaque hardens to become tartar.*

vitamin D: *A vitamin found in some foods, especially dairy foods. It is needed for healthy teeth and bones. Your body needs sunlight to use vitamin D properly.*

X-ray: *A type of photograph that shows hidden things such as bones in the body.*

To find out more...

...read these books

● Gaff, Jackie. *Why Must I Brush My Teeth?* Cherrytree Books, 2005.

● Moffatt, Julia. *Open Wide!* (Zig Zag Readers). The Evans Publishing Group, 2004.

● *Look After Yourself* KS2 CD Rom. Evans Publishing Group, 2006.

● Llewellyn, Claire. *Look After Yourself: Your Teeth*. Franklin Watts, 2002.

● Royston, Angela. *Healthy Teeth*. Heinemann Library, 2003.

● www.simplyteeth.com
Dental information for adults and children for healthy teeth and gums.

● www.bbc.co.uk/health/conditions/toothdecay2.shtml – Information from the BBC Health website on dental decay.

Index
Which page is it on?